*In the Canadian Heroes Series*

Glenn Gould–The Genius and His Music

Maureen Forrester–Canada's Charming Contralto

Three Caribbean Women in Canadian Politics

Dr. Robert Schemenauer–The Fog Catcher

# THREE CARIBBEAN WOMEN IN CANADIAN POLITICS

## A Biography for Young People

Lynette Roy
Edited by Hanna Miller

CANADIAN HEROES SERIES
Printed and bound by University of Toronto Press Inc.

© 2000 University of Toronto Press Incorporated
Toronto  Buffalo  London
Printed in Canada

ISBN 0-9684099-5-4
ISBN 0-9684099-8-9  (poster)

∞

Printed on acid-free paper

**Canadian Cataloguing in Publication Data**

Roy, Lynette, date
  Three Caribbean women in Canadian politics :
  a biography for young people

  (Canadian heroes series)
  Includes bibliographical references and index.
  ISBN 0-9684099-5-4
  ISBN 0-9684099-8-9  (poster)

  1. Augustine, Jean, 1937-    — Juvenile literature.
  2. Cools, Anne — Juvenile literature.
  3. Fry, Hedy, 1941-    — Juvenile literature.
  4. Women legislators — Canada — Biography — Juvenile literature.
  5. Caribbean-Canadian women — Biography — Juvenile literature.*
  6. Black Canadians — Biography — Juvenile literature.*

  I.  Miller, Hanna.
  II.  Title.
  III. Series: Canadian heroes series (Uxbridge, Ont.).

FC601.A1R69 2000
F1034.3.A2R69 2000
j328.71'0922
C00-930463-0

*This book is dedicated
to women of colour
who have contributed to politics in Canada
during the twentieth century and beyond.*

# CONTENTS

# FOREWORD

In 1979, I completed a study of Ontario high school girls. Fifty percent of those girls did not know any women who had the same careers that they had chosen. Times have changed. In 2000, young women have role models in many occupations. These role models inspire them to set and achieve goals for themselves.

Dr. Jean Augustine, M.P., Senator Anne C. Cools, and Hedy Fry, M.D., M.P. are role models for young people. These women are also emigrants from the Caribbean. As Canadian citizens, they have a strong commitment to work, a keen sense of justice, and respect for all peoples. These female politicians demonstrate that success can be achieved in Canada if we pursue our goals.

These three women are strong and courageous. It is not surprising that they have high academic records and that they have chosen political careers.

They have extended their humanitarian roles to include nation building in Canada.

Each of these women has succeeded in reducing injustices in Canadian society. They are now a part of the decision-making process. They have been involved in the design of legislation that promotes the progress of women, the poor, children, and fathers. They are human rights advocates.

These women have had personal challenges, yet they have remained strong and committed politicians. They have also remained loyal to their Caribbean roots.

Excellence and greatness are words that I use to describe these women. As William Arthur Ward said, "Greatness is not found in possessions, power, position, or prestige. It is discovered in goodness, humility, service, and character."

I salute Dr. Jean Augustine, M.P., Senator Anne C. Cools, and Hedy Fry, M.D., M.P. for being Canadian heroes.

*Dr. Avis Glaze*
*Associate Director of Education*
*York Region District School Board*
*Aurora, Ontario*

# INTRODUCTION AND ACKNOWLEDGEMENTS

Women from the Caribbean have been involved in Canadian politics for decades during the twentieth century. In 1972, Rosemary Brown became the first African Canadian woman of Jamaican ancestry to be elected to provincial politics. Many other women have worked behind the scenes, in political parties and in supportive roles, such as former Toronto Councillor Beverley Salmon and former Citizenship Judge Pamela Appelt.

The *Canadian Heroes Series* explores the lives of Canadians who have excelled in their chosen careers. Dr. Jean Augustine, M.P., Senator Anne C. Cools, and Hedy Fry, M.D., M.P. are Canadian heroes. Their life stories are interesting and they come from diverse family backgrounds, but their roles as leaders in Canadian politics unite them.

In doing my research on these and other dynamic women of colour, I have discovered many examples of heroism. Mary Ann Shadd pioneered the education in Canada of freed slaves and their children, and Harriet Tubman was the courageous leader of the Underground Railroad. I am convinced that these two women would have been proud of the subjects of this book because they embody the hopes and dreams of the "freedom seekers."

I am grateful to Jean Augustine, Anne Cools, and Hedy Fry for agreeing to be in the *Canadian Heroes Series*. I was overwhelmed by their generosity in providing personal photographs.

Thanks to my colleagues, Hanna Miller and Carol Tennent, for their support. Special thanks to Candace Clarke, assistant to Senator Anne C. Cools; Carole Nesbeth, legislative assistant to Dr. Jean Augustine, M.P.; and Tasleem Juma and Anna Maria Tosso, assistants to Hedy Fry, M.D., M.P. These women provided information for my research.

Special thanks to University of Toronto Press; Molly Schlosser for the production of this book and Val Cooke for her design.

*Lynette Roy*
*Uxbridge, Ontario*

# THREE CARIBBEAN WOMEN IN CANADIAN POLITICS

Dr. Jean Augustine, M.P.

# 1 DR. JEAN AUGUSTINE, M.P.

*Growing Up in Grenada*

Jean was born on September 9, 1937, in Happy Hill, Grenada, five kilometres from the capital St. George's. Ossie and Olive Simon were delighted with their first child. She had a sweet face, sparkling eyes, and a full head of black hair. She snuggled into her mother's arms.

Jean was nine months old when her father died of tetanus after a dental extraction. This sudden tragedy left Jean's mother with funeral expenses, an infant, and another baby on the way. Family and friends offered emotional support. Olive Simon's adoptive mother was a great help to the family at that time. Later, when Jean was old enough to speak, she called this lady Granny.

Olive had a second baby girl. Jean and her little sister grew up as close friends. At eleven, Jean won a scholarship to attend St. Joseph's Convent

Catholic High School. She looked smart in her navy pleated skirt, white blouse, and navy tie. At St. Joseph's, Jean was taught the Catholic principles of service to God and to people. The importance of helping those who were in need was also taught. Jean accepted these rules and volunteered to work in her parish. She helped the sick, taught children to read and write, and wrote letters for those people who were unable to write for themselves. Jean was also a member of the school's debating team.

Jean read constantly. She read historical novels as well as the classics. When she graduated from high school, Jean accepted a teaching position at St. Joseph's. She taught Grades One and Two, and her salary was $22 a month. Jean focused on the Three Rs: reading, writing, and arithmetic. She also taught at home, on Saturday mornings, people who had not completed their elementary education.

When Jean's mother remarried and went to live in Trinidad, Jean remained in Grenada. Having friends at church and at school influenced her decision, but it was Granny's presence that really made Jean want to stay there. Some of Jean's friends were planning to immigrate to Canada. The idea of pursuing a Canadian post-secondary education began to occupy her thoughts.

Granny encouraged Jean to follow her dream. When Jean first applied to immigrate to Canada on the Domestic Scheme, her application was denied because she had no work experience. Her second application was successful, however, and Jean traded her close community ties in the tropic for the unknown in a foreign land.

On May 24, 1960, Jean left Grenada for Canada, via Barbados. Her suitcase was packed with farewell presents from her neighbours and her students. The hardest part of all was saying goodbye to Granny. They hugged each other and, as tears were running down her cheeks, Granny said, "Girl, there is nothing you can't do. Go raise the family nose." Three carloads of people came to the airport to say goodbye. As her friends crowded around her, Jean said, "I'll never forget you all ... I'll write to everybody."

### A New Life in Canada

The airplane landed in Montreal, and Jean spent the night at the YWCA. The next day, she left by train for Toronto, where her new family and employer would meet her. This family had plans to spend the summer at their cottage, so Jean asked to work with another family. Her new employers were a doctor, his wife, and their baby son. The agreement was that Jean would work for this family for one year. In preparation for the future, Jean attended classes at night so that she would be admitted to university. Her employers encouraged Jean's dedication and helped her to get off in time for evening classes.

Jean spent her days off preparing assignments, but she also socialized with her friends. She wrote to her friends in Grenada and especially to Granny. Sometimes, when Jean felt homesick, a letter from Granny or from one of Jean's friends would make her feel happy again. Meanwhile, a baby girl was added to her employers' family.

At the end of the year, Jean got a job in the accounting department of Physicians' Services Inc. In her new role, she was responsible for taking care of invoices sent in by doctors. After work, she would return to her former employers' home. They provided Jean with room and board in return for her babysitting their two children.

In the fall of 1963, Jean was admitted to teachers' college. She had a busy schedule of working, going to school, and preparing assignments. She earned good grades, and when she graduated in the spring of 1964, Jean accepted a job at St. Anthony's Catholic School, in Toronto.

Jean continued her education at the University of Toronto, and earned the degrees of Bachelor of Arts, in 1973, and Master of Education, in 1980. Jean continued to take courses that helped her to be a good educator as well as a qualified teacher. The beneficiaries were her students, as she challenged them to focus on their school work and to aim for academic excellence.

### Jean Starts a Family

In spite of her busy schedule of upgrading her education and working as a teacher, Jean found time for romance, and soon wedding bells were ringing. Jean married Winston Augustine on June 29, 1968. They had a daughter in 1970 and another daughter in 1973. Jean was now responsible for several jobs: wife, mother, and educator. She regarded each of her roles as a part of her achievement as a woman. Jean enjoyed the role of mother most of all, with the help of a babysitter. Jean spent time reading to her daughters. She also encouraged self-expression and independence in her children.

### Community Involvement

Jean's drive for personal achievement did not hinder her commitment to others. She got involved in the Black community, when she came to Canada. Bromley Armstrong, a former member of the Ontario Labour Relations Board, recalled that Jean had taught Black children who were having problems at school. Jean understood the needs of immigrant families. Armstrong added that Jean had helped many Caribbean immigrants to adjust to Canadian society. In fact, an organization to help emigrants from Grenada to socialize and to establish themselves in Canada began in Jean's apartment. This organization is known as the Grenada Association.

In 1967, a committee was organized by Caribbean Canadians to celebrate Canada's Centennial. Its focus was on Caribbean music, art, dance, cuisine, and culture. Jean was involved with this first committee, and this celebration became known as Caribana.

After having worked as Vice-Principal, Jean was promoted to Principal at St. Felix Catholic School, a senior elementary school in Etobicoke, Ontario. Five years later, she became Principal at St. Gregory Catholic School, also in Etobicoke. Jean's students said that she was "the best teacher in the world." Her sensitivity, to children and especially to the needs of immigrants, compelled her to do community work. Jean encouraged

West Indian parents to become involved in their children's education. She became a role model for many Black parents in the community.

Jean's involvement extended beyond the Black community. She was a Trustee of the Hospital for Sick Children and served on the York University Board of Governors and on the Board of Harbourfront. Jean was a member of the Boards of the Urban Alliance on Race Relations; the Ontario Judicial Council; and the Etobicoke Social Development Council. Jean also worked to effect social change on the Boards of the Catholic Children's Aid Society; the Canadian Advisory Council on the Status of Women; as well as the Metropolitan Toronto Action Committee on Public Violence Against Women and Children.

Jean has served on municipal task forces on drug abuse and crime. As National President of the Congress of Black Women of Canada, Jean was regarded by her associates as a reserved but competent and hard-working leader.

In the spring of 1985, then Premier of Ontario David Peterson brought a team of "the brightest and the best" to help his government make the transition from Opposition to the governing party. Jean was a member of the transition team. She worked on the subcommittees and demonstrated her managerial skills. Politics came naturally to Jean, who enjoyed problem solving and team work.

In 1986, Jean received the YWCA's Women of Distinction Award for Community Service. Jean's name has been listed in the *Canadian Who's Who* yearly since 1987.

Mr. Peterson appointed Jean to be Chair of the Board of the Metropolitan Toronto Housing Authority in 1988. The housing authority addresses the challenges facing single-parent families and those families whose rent is based on income. Jean proved to be an excellent negotiator. When she resigned in May of 1993, to run for federal politics, Jean wrote *Accomplishments*, a 300-page report on the housing authority. Her colleagues agreed that there had been many accomplishments during her tenure; the most important having been an anti-drug strategy.

*Political Life*

Jean's experience as a community worker, her un-tiring ability to help people in need, and her inter-personal skills made her a politician-in-waiting. Jean was asked by several political parties to be a candidate at election time, but she always said that she wanted to be prepared. She wanted to be financially secure before running for public office. Jean's history of success was due, in part, to her never having accepted a job she could not handle.

When the election was called in 1993, Jean was appointed to run for the Liberal Party of Canada in the Etobicoke-Lakeshore riding. Many former students, their parents, and people in the community helped Jean with her campaign. She canvassed hard under the Liberal banner.

On October 24, 1993, the voters gave Jean a landslide victory over incumbent Progressive Conservative Patrick Boyer. A post-election party that Jean hosted included many Blacks who had travelled to celebrate her victory. Political history was made, that day, as Jean Augustine became the first Black woman to be elected as a federal Member of Parliament in Canada.

In 1960, then Prime Minister Lester B. Pearson asked a young politician named Jean Chrétien to be his Parliamentary Secretary. In 1993, when Mr. Chrétien formed the government, he asked Jean to be his Parliamentary Secretary. This meant that she would assist the Prime Minister with his parliamentary responsibilities. Jean felt honoured to be Prime Minister Jean Chrétien's Parliamentary Secretary.

Jean, as well as all the other Members of Parliament, found accommodations in Ottawa. While Parliament is in session, Jean lives in Ottawa and travels to her home in Etobicoke on weekends. She spends one week a month in her Etobicoke-Lakeshore office. Her schedule in Ottawa is hectic. She gets up at six in the morning and is in her office at eight. Meetings begin at half past eight. Question Period, committee meetings, House duty, and appointments fill the day. Lunch is usually a snack while doing other jobs. She returns home at nine in the evening or later, with material that must be prepared for the following morning.

When Jean sits behind the Prime Minister in the House of Commons, she is aware of her responsibilities. Jean believes that a Member of Parliament has the privilege of making the concerns of Canadians known. As a result, changes in Canadian society are brought about by the introduction of new legislation and/or changes in existing legislation.

Jean is grateful to her constituents for sending her to Ottawa to be their representative.

## THE HOUSE OF COMMONS

The House of Commons is the law-making system in Canada. There are 301 members: one from each riding or constituency. Candidates who win the largest number of votes in the general election are elected to be their ridings' representatives in the House of Commons. These ridings are in the ten provinces, the Northwest Territories, the Yukon Territory, and Nunavut.

### The Prime Minister

The Prime Minister is a Member of the House of Commons. Non-Members holding office would have to be elected to seats within a few months. The Prime Minister is the head of the political party and of the elected Members of Parliament. She/he presides over First Ministers' Conferences and government policy sessions, and receives Heads of State from foreign countries.

### The Governor General

The Prime Minister is appointed by the Governor General. The political party that wins the majority of seats during a general election forms the government. The leader of that party is asked by the Governor General to become Prime Minister. The Governor General may call on the Leader of the Opposition to form a new government, if one of the following two situations exists: 1. The Opposition wins more than half the seats in an election; or 2. The Government is defeated in the House of Commons and resigns.

Jean also remembers the two women who contributed much to her self-worth: Granny, who died in 1967, and Jean's mother, who has also died. Jean has said that they would have been proud "to know that I've come to this country and I've reached the highest place in the land."

### The Politician

During her first year in office, Jean spoke in the House of Commons on many issues, including the need for job creation. She was speaking on behalf of her constituents, because many of them had lost their jobs due to plant closures. Jean reminded her colleagues in Ottawa that Blacks had contributed to the growth of Canadian society. She also pointed out that the struggles and successes of Black Canadians had to be appreciated.

In April of 1994, Jean was a member of the Canadian delegation that was sent to observe the elections in South Africa. Upon her return to Canada, Jean reported her observations to the House of Commons. She said, "We determined the elections to be fair and free of intimidation and violence. A majority of the electorate was in a position to vote, and did so .... The South African people are to be congratulated for their tremendous achievement toward the goal of democracy."

In May of 1994, Jean headed a Canadian delegation to the Caribbean Development Bank's annual meeting in Belize, Central America. The purpose of attending this meeting was to speak on the Canadian position of support for the bank's work.

Jean's busy schedule was punctuated by a very special event. On June 16, 1994, an honourary Doctor of Laws degree was conferred on her at Convocation Hall by the University of Toronto. In her address to the convocation, Jean spoke of her appreciation of the past and of the present, as well as of her hope for the future. Jean said that her deceased mother and Granny would have been pleased to have been in attendance, that day. She went on to say that her mother had believed that "a doctor would raise the family nose", and that Granny would have said, "I knew you could do it. You deserve it!"

Jean offered the graduands five words that could lead to success: *"confidence, commitment, credibility, credentials,* and *community."* She told them that the pursuit of financial reward alone did not enhance the moral character of society. History, she said, had shown that this singular goal led to "social unrest."

Signing the register at convocation after receiving an honourary
Doctor of Laws degree from the University of Toronto (1994).
*Courtesy of the office of Dr. Jean Augustine, M.P.*

June 16 was also the United Nations' declared
Day of the African Child. Jean encouraged everyone to remember the children all over the world
who were suffering. In her tribute to Canada, Jean
said, "As a Canadian of Grenadian origin, I look
with pride to the fact that a number of us have
achieved a measure of success in Canadian
society." She added that, in this country, "race
or ethnic origin are not obstacles to fulfilling

one's goal." She went on to say, "Parliament is beginning to reflect the ethno-cultural diversity of our country ... these facts demonstrate Canada's credibility as the best country in the world to live [in]."

Jean concluded her address by saying that Canada was a leader in the world community. She suggested that we must contribute to other societies through the way we live and by setting high standards, which other nations can "strive to achieve."

### Parliamentary Secretary

Jean is a part of the decision-making process of Parliament. She has contributed to the modernization and restructuring of Canada's social programs. She was Vice-Chair of the Ministerial Task Force on Social Security Reform chaired by Minister Lloyd Axworthy. She was a member of the House of Commons Standing Committee on Human Resource Development. This committee travelled across the country to consult with Canadians. Jean was also involved in debates on several government reforms, including Bill C-41. This law requires the registration of guns and restricts the sale of firearms.

Jean copes with her assignments and accepts the challenges with the competent help of staff in her constituency office and on Parliament Hill. Her legislative and special assistants help her to organize her speaking engagements, maintain contact with her constituents, and entertain visitors from abroad.

When Princess Stella Sigcan, South Africa's Minister of Public Enterprises, came to Canada in search of investment for her country, Jean hosted a luncheon in Toronto for her. The two women encouraged and supported each other. Princess Stella said in her address that, with goodwill from the Canadian public, prayers, and investment, "we'll succeed."

Jean chaired a conference in Paris, France, from October 4 to 6, 1994. The aim of "Women in the City: Housing, Services and Urban Environment" was to empower women to participate in their countries' decision-making processes. It was arranged by the Secretary General of the Organisation for Economic Co-operation and Development (OECD). In preparing for the conference, Jean recalled her experiences as a community member and organizer. She told her colleagues in Paris that the issues related to women in urban society actually affected everyone. She added that resolving these issues would benefit women, men, and children. Jean said that women must participate before the decisions that will affect them are made. She suggested that their participation might be either as professionals or as consultants.

Jean informed the audience that, in Canada, women were taking responsibility for many important issues that affected them. One of these issues was housing, such as forms of transitional housing, including shelters. She stressed the need to focus on issues such as "urban affairs, women in the economy, and development aid."

The proceedings at this conference contributed to two events involving the OECD. The first of these was the 1995 United Nations Conference on the Status of Women. The second event was the United Nations Conference on Human Settlement, called Habitat 1996.

### *From Happy Hill to Parliament Hill*

One of the most unforgettable experiences that Jean has had took place in her home village in Grenada. She was on a short holiday to Grenada in 1994. To her surprise, a Grenadian government delegation met her at the airport. She received flowers and greetings from the people of Grenada. Jean was invited to have lunch with the Governor General, and was introduced to many Ministers in the Grenadian government.

Two days later, a reception in her village of Happy Hill was attended by two thousand people. Jean's cousin Dr. Keith Mitchell, who is, at present, the Prime Minister of Grenada, presented Jean with a wooden plaque at the end of the ceremony. The plaque, which is in Jean's office in Ottawa, has these memorable words engraved on it: *From Happy Hill to Parliament Hill*. This plaque reminds Jean that her family and friends in Grenada are proud of her achievements.

Another memorable event occurred one day as Jean left the House of Commons. A reporter pursued her down the stairs while calling her by name. Jean stopped to find out what she wanted to know. The reporter did not have a question, but her statement startled Jean. She identified herself as the sister of the toddler whom Jean had cared for when she first came to Canada. Jean's eyes filled with tears as she admired the beautiful young woman standing beside her.

Jean is aware of her role as a forerunner to future Black politicians. She appreciates the fact that she can do a small part of the work that needs to be done. However, she aims for excellence as she represents herself and her constituents in Ottawa.

The message that Jean sends to aspiring young politicians and to other young people is, "It's not where you're coming from but where you're going to that's important." Jean believes this statement because it is the story of her life.

On December 14, 1995, Jean stood on the floor of the House of Commons and asked for unanimous consent to a motion by Parliament. In response to a request that she had received from the Ontario Black History Society, Jean asked that February be declared Black History Month across Canada. The motion was unanimously passed, affirming the role that people of African descent have made in Canada. It states: "That this House take note of the important contributions of Black Canadians to the settlement, growth and development of Canada, the diversity of the Black community in Canada and its importance in the history of the country, and recognize February as Black History Month."

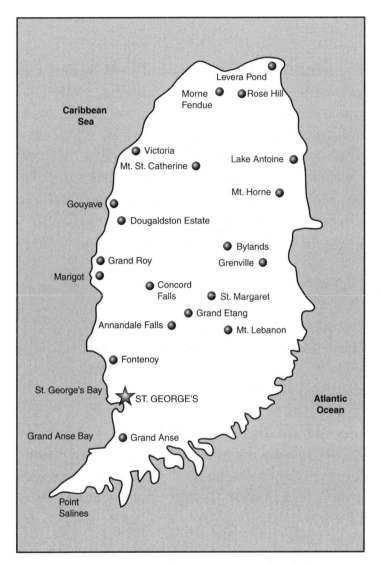

**GRENADA**

## GRENADA

The most southern of the Windward Islands has hills with dense forests, many streams, waterfalls, and rivers. Grenada, Carriacou, and Petite Martinique combine to form a three-island independent state within the Commonwealth. Its area measures 340 sq. km (131 sq. mi.). It has a population of 97,008. St. George's is Grenada's capital and a delightful harbour town. It is set against a backdrop of steep hills, red roofs, and winding roads.

*Climate*

The average temperature in Grenada is 27°C (80°F). The rainy season is from June to December.

*History and Government*

Grenada was discovered by Christopher Columbus in 1498. During the colonial years in the eighteenth century, Grenada changed ownership between Britain and France. Britain finally claimed it in 1784.

The Queen of England is the Queen of Grenada and the Head of State. She is represented by the Governor General. The Prime Minister is the head of the government.

*Economy*

Grenada is the Caribbean's spice island. One-third of the world's nutmeg is produced there. Other spices that are grown in Grenada are: mace, ginger, cloves, cinnamon, and coriander. These spices are picked, sorted, dried, and packed for export by the local people. Grenadians live close to the land and are dedicated to their spice groves.

Grenadians also enjoy the sea, and their fishing villages are vibrant and happy places. The island has abundant fruit trees, which are laden with colourful fruit such as mangoes, guavas, and soursops.

*Tourism*

Tourism boosts the Grenadian economy, and Grenadians are hospitable people. Late July and early August are the most festive times in Grenada and Carriacou. Three major celebrations overlap: the Carriacou Regatta, the Rainbow City Festival, and Grenada Carnival. These festivals are accompanied by shows, races, competitions, parades, exhibits, and pageants.

Grenada has excellent beaches, sailing, and diving conditions. Grand Anse Beach is one of the most beautiful beaches in the Caribbean. The

Easter Regatta attracts yachts from many countries to the coasts of Grenada. Petite Martinique is famous for boat building and fishing.

Nature enthusiasts and adventure seekers visit Grenada because of its hiking trails and bird-watching. One-sixth of the island is reserved for national parks and bird sanctuaries. Humpback whales can be seen off the coasts of Grenada and Carriacou during their migration from December to April.

*Education*

Grenadians have a high standard of education. St. George's University Medical School in Grenada is a part of St. George's University Medical School in New York City.

Senator Anne C. Cools

# 2 SENATOR ANNE C. COOLS

## *Growing Up in Barbados*

She was born in 1943 on St. Clare's Day, August 12, in Barbados, West Indies. Her father, Lucius, and her mother, Rosita, were delighted to have another daughter. She was a big baby, at fifteen pounds. They named her Anne Clare. Anne was born into a large family with grandparents, aunts, uncles, cousins, and siblings. They all showered her with love and affection.

The Millers and the Cools were entrepreneurs and contributed to the economy of Barbados. Some family members owned an ice factory. Others were involved in food processing and food export. The family owned land, and some family members were politicians.

Anne's mother, Rosita Cools (*née* Miller), owned a sugar cane plantation. Rosita's father, Luther Miller, was a municipal politician as well as an exporter of tamarind. Anne's Uncle Fredrick was Minister of Health and Social Services during the mid 1950s.

---

**TAMARIND**

This tropical fruit has a plump brown pod and soft brown pulp. The pulp of the tamarind is used in the production of Asian sauces, canned fruit, and medicines.

---

Anne's father, Lucius Cools, was a pharmacist. Before Anne was born, her father had been a candidate in the Barbadian general election of 1938. Although he lost that election, Lucius Cools had made significant contributions to the early development of the political party called the Progressive Conservative League. He helped in the planning and organizing of political meetings. The Progressive League became the Barbados Labor Party (BLP) in 1938 and was led by its founder, Sir Grantley Adams. The BLP is currently one of three major political parties in Barbados.

*Young Anne*

Lucius and Rosita watched in amazement as Anne grew into a toddler. She began to speak and to read before her second birthday. Anne blossomed into a healthy child. She spoke eloquently, especially when she needed to explain what she wanted. Anne's parents admired her mannerisms and her zeal for life, and they told her repeatedly that she was special.

Anne's long arms and legs earned her the nickname "Dog Bones." Anne knew that this was not meant to be derogatory. She knew that she was loved by her family. Anne and her brothers and sisters played rounders (which is similar to baseball), hide-and-seek, and cricket. Her long legs made running easy, and she could run as fast as her older brothers could.

Anne was a sensitive child who would cry alone if she felt hurt. When she was four years old, a tragedy occurred in her family. One of Anne's older brothers died of peritonitis, which is an infection of the membrane that lines the abdomen. It was difficult for Anne to bear her beloved brother's funeral service. It was also painful for her to watch her family grieve.

Within a year, one of Anne's younger sisters also died of peritonitis. Anne saw her mother weeping for her lost children. Anne became so distraught by the extreme sadness and suffering of her family that her speech pattern regressed. This once talkative child became quiet and spoke only in monosyllables. Her speech returned to normal gradually, over the next year.

The effect of the deaths of her siblings has never left Anne's memory. She has grappled with the loss of her siblings as she has tried to accept it. This experience has helped her to realize that the greatest tragedy for a parent is the loss of a child. Anne's sensitivity to hurt and pain has made her a compassionate human being.

*World Events*

Anne grew up in Barbados at the end of World War II. At that time, governments all over the world were restructuring. These were also the days before television in Barbados. Radio newscasts from Europe were broadcast by the BBC (British Broadcasting Corporation). Anne paid attention to world events, and her parents discussed these events with their children. She became aware of the names of world leaders, such as Archbishop Makarios III of Greece, Dr. Eric Williams of Trinidad and Tobago, and Prime Minister Lester B. Pearson of Canada.

Anne's formative years were influenced mostly by her family, but also by her education and by her perception of the world. At school, Anne often debated world events and Barbadian politics in class. She was a Girl Guide and was regarded by her peers as an expert on local and foreign events.

### The Canadian Experience

The Cools family immigrated to Montreal in groups between 1955 and 1957. Anne and her mother arrived together. Anne was a teenager when she came to Canada and, because she knew a lot about world events, she was a well-informed newcomer. Anne knew that the Commonwealth included Canada and the Caribbean. She saw her new status in Canada as a Barbadian who had moved from one part of the British Empire to another.

Anne attended Thomas d'Arcy McGee High School. On weekends and during the summer holidays she worked at Reddy Memorial Hospital. Later on, she worked in the laboratory at Montreal General Hospital. Anne enrolled at McGill University to earn a Bachelor of Arts degree.

In the summer of 1963, she toured Europe. She was saddened when she saw the paintings of war and the headstones on the graves. Anne observed the names and ages of some of the young people who had died during World War II. She noticed that some of these young people had been her age or younger when they died. These realities activated her social conscience and made Anne feel intense anger. Anne returned to Canada with a passion to change the world.

### A Personal Statement for Justice

In 1966, six students had made a complaint about racism to the administration office at Sir George Williams University (now Concordia University). These complaints had not been addressed, and a demonstration was planned. The students decided to occupy the English Department. Anne agreed to be a part of the sit-in and joined the group. This was her opportunity to speak for justice.

An unknown group of students changed the plan and proceeded to damage the computer centre at the university. The riot squad, in full gear, arrived at the campus and surrounded the building that the students had occupied. Anne was arrested along with the other students. This demonstration, which had started as an act of civil disobedience, had become a nightmare.

After having had her fingerprints and mug shots taken, Anne was released on $25,000 bail.

Four years later, the trial began and Anne, her lawyer, and her parents entered the courtroom. Anne's family believed in her innocence. However, at the end of three weeks, she was found guilty. Anne maintained her innocence (as she had been part of the peaceful protest) and refused to confess to any wrongdoing. She also refused to plea bargain. Anne was sent to jail for four months. The other students received various jail sentences.

While in prison, Anne had time to reflect on her life, her wonderful parents, her disciplined upbringing, and her future. When she felt depressed, she would pray, meditate, read, or do yoga. Being in jail was a humiliating experience for Anne. She planned to continue helping people when she was discharged. She was also determined to live a good life beyond the jail cell.

The injustices of life, the jail sentence, and the consequences of struggling for change have given Anne wisdom and empathy. Some people have taunted Anne about her jail sentence. Although it is hurtful to be reminded of this past indignity, Anne is a courageous woman who defies her critics by standing tall. She has put this experience into perspective and regards it as a learning experience.

Anne applied for a pardon for her conviction of willful obstruction. She attempted to prove that the system works. In 1981, Anne was granted the pardon by the National Parole Board of Canada. This provided Anne with emotional release and the motivation to pursue her personal goals.

### Aiming for the Top Job

Anne worked as a field instructor. She was employed by the University of Toronto, in the Faculty of Social Work, from 1977 to 1978 and by Ryerson Polytechnic Institute (now Ryerson Polytechnic University), from 1978 to 1980. She joined Seneca College in 1977 and worked there until 1989.

As Field Instructor, Anne was responsible for supervising students and training them to be competent social workers. One of the skills that Anne taught her students was how to be good listeners. Anne and her students were very concerned about violence in society. They became increasingly aware of domestic violence and its impact on women and children. Anne realized that, in order to comprehend the various factors of domestic violence, men had to be included in the dialogue and in counselling.

A place where women and their children could find shelter during times of domestic violence became one of Anne's dreams. In 1974, that dream became a reality when Anne founded Women in Transition, Inc. Its mission was to move family members from their harmful home environments to a place of shelter. Then counselling would include the husband as well as the wife. Reconciliation was supported as an option. The home was funded by the Ontario government and the United Way. According to Dr. W. Gunther Plaut, a local rabbi, there was enough work for seven full-time workers and thirty-five volunteers. He said, "This house at 143 Spadina Road is quite a place, and I came away from it feeling very good indeed."

In 1978, Anne ran for public office as she attempted to give the problem of domestic violence a more public profile. She sought the nomination for the Liberal Party in Rosedale, but lost to John Evans, who was then President of the University of Toronto. In 1979, Anne won the nomination, but lost the election to former Mayor of Toronto David Crombie. This defeat was hard for her to take, and she had a great deal of difficulty accepting the rejection. Anne wanted very much to be an elected Member of Parliament.

As Executive Director of Women in Transition, Inc., Anne continued to be a motivating force to her staff and a source of encouragement to the women who needed shelter. Anne also served on several committees in the Toronto area.

Anne was a member of the Board of Directors of the Black Education Project, Black Theatre Canada, the Pauline McGibbon Cultural Centre, and the Social Planning Council of Metropolitan Toronto. She was Founding Vice-Chair and Executive Committee Member of the Metropolitan Toronto Justice Committee on Spousal Abuse. She served as a Member of the National Parole Board of Canada from 1980 to 1984. Anne gave each role the Cools touch of excellence.

### Excellence Has Its Rewards

Anne Clare Cools made Canadian political history in January of 1984 when she was summoned to the Senate of Canada by then Governor General Edward Schreyer. The appointment was made on the advice of then Prime Minister Pierre Elliott Trudeau.

Anne recalls the day that the message came to her, first by telephone. She was surprised by the appointment and, although she had always wanted to be an elected Member of Parliament, she liked the idea of being a Senator. She knew that the Senate was the place where decisions in Canada were ratified. She was also convinced that, as a Senator, she should give the issue of domestic violence a national voice.

The appointment was printed in every major newspaper across the country. Some people felt that Anne was making a compromise because of the security of a good annual salary and a pension. These critics also suggested that, if Anne truly wanted to effect social change, then the Senate was not the place for her. Other critics regarded the appointment by Mr. Trudeau before he left office as being one of Black tokenism. These criticisms did not discourage Anne, because she knew that she could make a difference. Her motto, Excellence is its own reward, seemed to make more sense as she contemplated the move to Ottawa.

Anne is blessed with friends and supporters, and they came to her defence. Her colleagues at Women in Transition, Inc. lauded the appointment and believed that she deserved to be a Senator. Bromley Armstrong, a leader in the Black community, said that Anne was qualified for the job. He added that the appointment of a Black person to the Senate was timely.

The new Senator said that she was the ideal choice for the job, based on her excellent track record in serving the public. She indicated that service to the public would be her goal as a Senator.

### Senator Anne Clare Cools

Anne began as a full-fledged member of the Senate. In 1990, she served as a member of the Special Senate Committee on Bill C-62, the Act to implement the Goods and Services Tax (GST). Anne represents Ontario in the Senate. In 1993, she was elected Vice-Chair of the Greater Toronto Liberal Caucus.

When Jean Chrétien and the Liberal Party of Canada formed the government in 1993, the Liberal Senators became the Government Senators. After having been in Opposition for nine years, Anne and the other Senators were delighted to be on the Government side. On January 18, 1994, then Governor General Raymond Hnatyshyn delivered the Speech from the Throne in the Senate Chamber. In the audience were former Prime Minister Pierre Elliott Trudeau, other Privy Councillors, former government Ministers, and members of the faith communities. Anne described this event as a "great moment in history", and added, "I felt blessed to have been part of it." She was asked to perform the task of seconding the motion on the Senate debate on the Speech from the Throne.

On January 19, 1994, Anne seconded the motion on the Senate debate by pledging support for the government's program. She reminded her colleagues that Canada had produced many great Liberals. She also reminded them of the principles of Liberalism. Firstly, that the State and the government exist to serve the people; not to be served by the people. Secondly, that the family is the foundation of society. Thirdly, that self-government provides the best assurance that the State will promote welfare, the individual, and the family. Anne endorsed Prime Minister Chrétien's motto: He serves most who leads. She added that support for the government was critical if its policies were to be implemented. She closed her speech by saying, "Honourable Senators, we place our program before this Chamber and ask all Honourable Senators to support it."

*The Senate On Domestic Violence*

Anne has been involved with issues pertaining to family conflict and family violence for most of her adult life. She considers violence in the family to be such a traumatic experience that it should never be ignored. She is also aware that the effect of violence on children is that they will display the same behaviour. Her experience as Executive Director of Women in Transition, Inc. has given her insight into this pattern of behaviour.

On March 28, 1995, Anne addressed the Senate on the problem of violence in society. She began by recalling two visionaries who had changed the way society regarded illness. Firstly, Dr. Philippe Pinel (1745-1826), who had believed that the mentally ill should be cared for with respect. Secondly, Dr. Sigmund Freud (1856-1936), who had introduced the theory of neurosis and that painful experiences in life could have negative results.

Anne said that, in 1992, the rate of violent crime in Canada had doubled since 1977 and male offenders had been responsible for the majority of the violence. She also said that Canadians were preoccupied with their safety and security. Anne suggested that the high level of violence in society would never be curbed by building large prisons, hiring more police, or designing treatment programs for offenders. Anne believed that personal and community safety could only be achieved by identifying the "causal factors" that were connected to crime and violence.

Anne referred to that speech on March 7, 1995, which was International Women's Day. In her speech that day she said that, in order to comprehend male abuse, we must examine the childhood experience of the abusing male and his relationship with his mother. Anne suggested that child abuse inflicted by the mother contributed to the anger and violence in male adults. She added that mothers played a vital role in the emotional and mental health of their children.

Anne pointed out that it was difficult to define and identify some forms of child abuse. She referred to the *Lalonde Report* of 1976, which included the neglected child, as well as the physically and emotionally abused child, as cause for concern. This report suggested that child battering was "the tip of the iceberg of child abuse and neglect." Anne addressed other issues of child abuse, from Dickens's *Oliver Twist* to the present, to show that child neglect and child abuse were neither new nor inseparable.

Anne's comprehensive overview was applauded by her colleagues in the Senate. However, her association between violent males and their relationships with their mothers made many feminists angry. Her comments were contrary to these feminists' ideologies and the feminists spoke loudly against the Senator's statements. Anne replied, "Now that you are outraged, you will start to think," and she said to the press, "Why, I thought everyone knew!" The confrontation following her speech made news across Canada, but the Senator was unrepentant.

Critics of Anne's ideas were loud, but so were her supporters. Dr. Cyril Greenland, a retired professor of social work at McMaster University, welcomed the debate sparked by Anne. His study of one hundred child deaths showed that mothers had murdered their children in thirty-nine cases and fathers had been guilty in thirteen cases. One study in the United States of America linked physical abuse by mothers and violent sex murders.

Dr. Nico Trocmé, a University of Toronto professor of social work and the author of a study on child abuse, explained that children were usually in the care of their mothers. He also said that fathers who were absent were also neglectful, because they had abandoned their children. He added that neglectful fathers were not usually included in some studies on child abuse.

Anne's comments brought the complex issue of child abuse to the public arena. The debate showed the divisions that existed among academics in their interpretation of statistics. Anne was encouraged by the telephone calls, faxes, and letters to her Ottawa office in support of her comments.

One supporter reminded Anne of an article that had been written by Rabbi Dr. W. Gunther Plaut in 1979, as proof of her knowledge of issues related to violence in the family. Anne had based her comments on several well-informed sources. One source was Dr. Robert ten Bensel, Director of Maternal and Child Health at the University of Minnesota. Dr. ten Bensel had advised a Canadian Senate Subcommittee that a boy who had been abused by his mother could become a sex murderer.

Another source that Anne referred to was a 1989 report by Health Canada. It said that child abuse was the only form of family violence that women were as guilty of as men. On *Morningside*, a Toronto-based radio show, the host once asked listeners which parent had been more abusive. Sixty percent of respondents identified their mothers as having been more abusive, while thirty-eight percent cited their fathers. Anne said that the data spoke on behalf of the children.

Anne's name has been listed in the *Canadian Who's Who* yearly since 1985. Her name has also been mentioned at the United Nations in New York, as well as in Munich and Geneva, with regard to her work on family violence. During the summer of 1998, a Canadian tourist in Germany was asked by a German politician about Senator Anne Cools. The politician commented on Senator Cools's work on the issue of families in crisis. He added, "You have an amazing Senator in your country."

---

**THE SENATE**

In 1867, the Fathers of Confederation designed the existing system of government for Canada. The Governor General is the Queen's representative in the upper House, or the Senate, as well as in the lower House, or the House of Commons.

The Senate consists of 105 seats: 24 from the Maritimes (10 from Nova Scotia, 10 from New Brunswick, and 4 from Prince Edward Island); 24 from Ontario; 24 from Quebec; 24 from the Western provinces (6 each from Manitoba, Saskatchewan, Alberta, and British Columbia); 6 from Newfoundland; and 1 each from the Yukon Territory, the Northwest Territories, and

Nunavut. In 1990, during the Free Trade debate, the Senate was increased. This was the first time that provision for four or eight extra Senators was used.

Senators are appointed by the Governor General on the advice of the Prime Minister. They can remain in office until age 75. However, if they have missed two consecutive sessions of Parliament, then they must resign. Senators must live in the province or territory that they represent.

Senators come from various lifestyles. For example: former hockey players, government Ministers, lawyers, Premiers, social workers, and farmers. They bring diverse skills to the Senate, and these skills help to make the Senate relevant to the issues of society.

Most of the work of the Senate is done in Committees, where Bills are examined clause by clause. The Senators listen to representatives from different groups that would be affected by a specific Bill. These Committees meet in Ottawa. They also travel across the country to meet Canadians. When the Senators make amendments to the Bills that have been passed by the House of Commons, their decisions are made after consultation with Canadians. These changes are usually accepted by the House of Commons.

The Senate can introduce any Bill, except for those concerning the spending of public money or taxes. Also, the Senate can improve or reject any Bill brought before a Committee. A Bill cannot become law unless it has been approved by the Senate.

In spite of its great power, the Senate has not rejected any Bills that were passed by the House of Commons over the past forty years. However, in 1988, the Senate refused to pass the Free Trade Agreement until it had been submitted to the Canadian people in the form of a general election. Also, in 1989 and 1990, the Senate recommended amendments to the Unemployment Insurance Bill. The House of Commons rejected the amendments and the Senate passed the Bill as it had been submitted. In 1991, the Senate defeated a Commons Bill on abortion.

Recently, the Senate has extended its role to include the investigation of poverty, child abuse, spouse abuse, unemployment, inflation, the elderly, Aboriginal affairs, and the efficiency of government departments. These investigations have produced informative reports and have led to changes in legislation and/or Government policy.

Senators have salaries and permanent staff, so their work in these areas is done at lower cost than the work of Royal Commissions or task forces.

## No Place Like Home

Anne Cools and Rolf Calhoun were married on March 22, 1986, at St. Olav's Anglican Church in Toronto. The officiating minister was Reverend Reginald Rose. The reception was held at their first home, in the Annex district of Toronto. Anne recalls that many people attended the wedding ceremony and the reception, in spite of the brisk March wind that day.

Anne and Rolf share many hobbies. One of these is cooking together. True enjoyment for them is a home-cooked meal, with the table set with their favourite dinnerware. They also enjoy dining together by candlelight. Anne and Rolf both love gardening. They have many indoor plants and, during the summer, their garden is spectacular with vegetables and flowers. Their home in Ottawa is a twenty-five-minute drive from Parliament Hill.

Anne travels across Canada with Senate Committees. When she returns home, Anne relaxes with her husband by listening to classical music. Their favourite composers are J.S. Bach, Beethoven, Handel, and Mozart. Anne takes music lessons and enjoys practising old and new scores on her piano. She uses music as therapy to relax after long sessions away from home or at the Senate.

The Holy Bible is one of Anne's favourite books. She is a member of the Ottawa branch of the Prayer Book Society of Canada. Anne finds in her sacred scriptures the strength she needs to be a wife and a Senator. She admits that there are many challenges in being a politician. For example, patience and tolerance are needed when dealing with the public. Also, she must be able to focus on an issue in spite of the criticism around her.

One of her favourite psalms is 127:3, "Children are a gift from the Lord; they are a real blessing." Anne believes that all people must overcome prejudice from within themselves. She has said, "Prejudice is a part of the darker side of human nature."

Anne is proud of her ancestors. There is a family history of politicians today and for three generations past. Anne believes that she will continue to be an effective leader in Canadian politics. The sources of her strength are God and her marriage.

As a Canadian, Anne's vision of Canada is that it is a humane and productive country. Her response to people who need help is, "I can help you," and "I want to encourage you."

*"Courage and trustworthiness are two of the most noble characteristics that we can possess."*

Senator Anne C. Cools

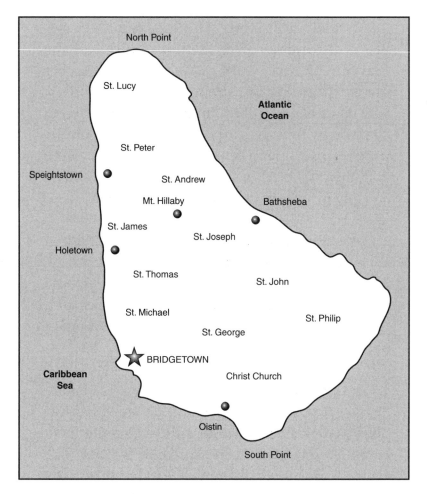

**BARBADOS**

## BARBADOS

The rough Atlantic Ocean pounds its north-east coast. The south-west coast is soothed by the calm Caribbean Sea. Barbados is the most easterly of the Caribbean Islands. Its area measures 430 sq. km (166 sq. mi.). It has a population of 259,191. Bridgetown is the capital of Barbados.

*Climate*

Barbados is windy because of the trade winds. It has low humidity even in the summer months. The average temperature in Barbados is 27°C (80°F). Rainfall keeps the trees green and lush. The rainy season is from June to November.

*History and Government*

In 1537, Portuguese sailors called the island *Los Barbados* because of the large number of ficus trees. These trees have long, dangling roots that look like beards. Modern Barbados is called Little England. Barbadians have embraced English law and traditions as a way of life for over three hundred and sixty years.

The first Parliament in Barbados was held in 1639. This island is the third-oldest member of the

Commonwealth. The oldest is the British House of Commons, in London. The second-oldest is the Bermuda House of Assembly, in Bermuda.

Barbados became an independent island within the Commonwealth on November 30, 1966. The Queen of England is the Queen of Barbados and the Head of State. She is represented by the Governor General. The Prime Minister is the head of the government.

*Economy*

The Barbadian economy is based on many sectors. These include tourism, light manufacturing, agriculture, fishing, and financial services.

Tourism drives the Barbadian economy. Sugar cane is the chief export. Farmers grow and export fruit, vegetables, poultry, and meat. Many foreign banks have branches on the island, providing employment for islanders. Two Canadian banks in Barbados are the Royal Bank of Canada and the Canadian Imperial Bank of Commerce (CIBC).

*Tourism*

Barbados is the port of call for many Caribbean cruises. The cruise ships dock at Port Barbados in Bridgetown. This bustling capital has many colonial buildings and thrives on its safety for tourists.

Tour guides are fluent in German, Spanish, French, and Italian. Tourists are enticed by marketplaces, craft shops, duty-free shopping, and beautiful beaches. Barbados has over seventy square miles of beaches, and the sand colours range from delicate pink to pure white.

*Sports*

Cricket is the national sport of Barbados. Many outstanding cricketers come from there and form the West Indies Cricket Team. Sir Garfield Sobers was knighted by Queen Elizabeth II for his contribution to cricket in the West Indies and around the world.

The climate of Barbados encourages participation in a wide range of sports, such as yachting and other water sports. Barbadians also enjoy long-distance running.

*Education*

Barbados has the highest standard of education in the Caribbean. The University of the West Indies campus at Cave Hill offers degrees in arts and sciences. The faculty of law is in Barbados.

The Parliament Building, Ottawa, Ontario. *Reproduced with the consent of the Library of Parliament.*

## THE RIGHT HONOURABLE
## PIERRE ELLIOTT TRUDEAU

When former Prime Minister Lester B. Pearson re-signed, Mr. Pierre Elliott Trudeau became the twentieth Prime Minister of Canada. He had won the Liberal Party of Canada leadership and had gone on to win the general election in 1968 with a solid majority government.

An editorial entitled, "The Importance of Mr. Trudeau" appeared in the Manchester *Guardian*: "The new Canadian Prime Minister, Mr. Pierre Trudeau, is a French Canadian. In the present tense climate of relations between the two com-munities in Canada, this is perhaps the most significant fact. Canada has had French-Canadian Prime Ministers before, but never at a time of such importance to the survival of the nation as today."

Mr. Trudeau also won general elections in 1972 and 1974. In 1979, the Liberal Party under his lead-ership lost the election to Mr. Joe Clark. Former Prime Minister Pierre Elliott Trudeau became the leader of the Opposition. Nine months later, then Prime Minister Joe Clark's Progressive Conservative government fell after a vote of non-confidence. Mr. Trudeau became Prime Minister again in 1980 until he announced his retirement from politics on

February 29, 1984, and left office on June 30 of that same year.

During his tenure, then Prime Minister Pierre Elliott Trudeau was a charismatic leader who renewed Canadians' optimism about their country. Mr. Trudeau was fluently bilingual, and his government made Canada an officially bilingual country. English and French became the official languages. The word "Trudeaumania" was coined to describe how Canadians adored Mr. Trudeau, and to convey the sense of pride that he had instilled in Canadians.

The press, television reporters, and world leaders were fascinated by then Prime Minister Trudeau's style of leadership. He had a youthful look, charm, and intelligence, which appealed to the public. Mr. Trudeau also had an endearing smile, and he kissed babies whenever he met them during his election campaigns. He dressed elegantly and wore a red rose in his lapel.

Then Prime Minister Pierre Elliott Trudeau married Margaret Joan Sinclair. They had three sons. Justin was born on Christmas Day in 1971; Sacha, on Christmas Day in 1973; and Michel, in October of 1975. Michel died in a skiing accident in 1998.

Many Canadians believed that Mr. Trudeau would solve the Quebec separatism issue. He coped with the separatists tactfully, and even declared that separatism was dead in Quebec. However, the separatists proved him wrong. They resurfaced and have waged many unsuccessful attempts to separate the province of Quebec from Canada.

Mr. Trudeau, who had been a law professor in Montreal before becoming a politician, used the law successfully to keep the separatists in line.

October of 1970 was the beginning of a sombre period in Canadian history called the October Crisis. The Front de Libération du Québec (FLQ) kidnapped British diplomat James Cross and Quebec Cabinet Minister Pierre Laporte. In response, then Prime Minister Pierre Elliott Trudeau's government invoked the emergency War Measures Act. This brought Canadian Armed Forces troops into the streets of Ottawa and Quebec. The soldiers had orders to arrest and detain without bail. Mr. Laporte was murdered in captivity, but law and order were eventually restored.

Mr. Trudeau has many critics. They describe him as a failure because he did not quash the separatists. However, former Prime Minister

Pierre Elliott Trudeau's legacy is one of personal freedom, individualism, and excellence. He has defied his critics.

According to opinion polls taken in 1999, Mr. Trudeau has emerged as one of the few past Prime Ministers who had vision and integrity. In an Angus Reid poll published in January of 2000, forty-three percent of respondents named Mr. Trudeau Prime Minister of the Century. Also that month, Mr. Trudeau was voted Newsmaker of the Century in a Canadian Press/Broadcast News poll of editors and broadcasters.

Former Prime Minister Trudeau's greatest contribution to the Canadian lifestyle was the *Canadian Charter of Rights and Freedoms*. Mr. Trudeau brought the Constitution of Canada from England to Canada in 1981. His government inserted the *Charter* into the Constitution. The section of the *Charter* called "Equality Rights" states, "Every individual is equal before and under the law .... "

The *Charter* had an immediate impact on the lives of Canadians. According to the *Charter*, the rights of the individual are not based on the collective rights of the population. Canadian courts use the *Charter* as a reference. Laws are passed and

The Right Honourable Pierre Elliott Trudeau. *Courtesy of Jean Marc Carisse, Photographer to the Prime Minister.*

judgements are made, based on the *Charter*. Canadian society is free because of the *Canadian Charter of Rights and Freedoms*.

The Right Honourable Pierre Elliott Trudeau celebrated his eightieth birthday on October 18, 1999. He works for a Montreal law firm. A reporter said that Mr. Trudeau can still walk into a room full of people and become the focus of everyone's attention. The fascination with former Prime Minister Trudeau lies in his passion for Canada. He loves this great country. He is a Canadian hero.

*"We must now establish the basic principles, the basic values and beliefs which hold us together as Canadians so that beyond our regional loyalties there is a way of life and a system of values which make us proud of the country that has given us such freedom and such im-measurable joy."*

Canadian Charter of Rights and Freedoms
The Rt. Hon. Pierre Elliott Trudeau
1981

*Reproduced with the permission of the Minister of Public Works and Government Services Canada, 1999.*

Hedy Fry, M.D., M.P.

# 3  HEDY FRY, M.D., M.P.

## The Early Years

Hedy Madeline Fry was born on August 6, 1941, in the oil refining town of San Fernando, Trinidad. Her parents were delighted with their daughter. Her grandmother, Rose Ferraz, thought that Hedy was the most beautiful baby.

As Hedy grew up and became aware of politics, her grandmother was her role model. Rose Ferraz was a social and political activist who was involved in church and social activities. Hedy remembers one of her grandmother's favourite sayings: "If you don't like what is happening, don't complain; go in and fix it." These words have influenced Hedy's view of her role as an instrument for change. Hedy's childhood dream was to be an international journalist.

Hedy's parents also influenced her life. Her father was a gentle and deeply spiritual man who taught Hedy compassion and faith. Her mother worked all her life. The principal at St. Joseph's Convent in San Fernando, Sister Francis Xavier, was a strong role model, as well. She impressed Hedy with her dynamism, outspokenness, and love of literature, beauty, and truth. In 1960, Hedy was Valedictorian of her graduating class.

## The Family Doctor

Hedy left Trinidad in 1961 to study medicine at the Royal College of Surgeons in Dublin, Ireland. During her years as a medical student, she directed plays and choreographed dances. Hedy excelled in applied physiology, for which she was awarded a silver medal in 1968.

After earning a medical degree, Hedy married Peter Fry. Their first son, named Peter, was born in Ireland in 1969. Then the Frys immigrated to Canada. Their second and third sons were born in Canada: Jeremy in 1972 and Douglas in 1974.

Hedy was a family practitioner at St. Paul's Hospital in Vancouver. During her practice, she delivered more than eight hundred babies. Hedy was President of the British Columbia Federation of Medical Women in 1977. She was President of the Vancouver Medical Association from 1988 to

1989. Hedy was also President of the British Columbia Medical Association from 1990 to 1991 and the chief negotiator for the physicians of British Columbia from 1990 to 1992.

In the late 1980s, Hedy was regularly featured on a television program called *DOCTOR, DOCTOR*, which was primarily concerned with the health of women, children, and seniors. This Canadian Broadcasting Corporation (CBC) medical magazine dealt with illness prevention, health promotion, self-care, and simplifying the understanding of illness.

Hedy's name was first listed in the *Canadian Who's Who* in 1996. It has appeared yearly since 1998.

### The Politician

Hedy worked on political campaigns. Federally, in 1984 for former Prime Minister John Turner; provincially, in 1990 for Art Cowie. She had chosen the Liberal Party of Canada because she agreed with the principles of Liberalism that said that the State and the government exist to serve the people with good public policy and programs.

Hedy was chosen to be a Liberal candidate for Member of Parliament in the general election

At Kitsilano Beach, in her riding of Vancouver-Centre. *Courtesy of the office of Hedy Fry, M.D., M.P.*

of October 25, 1993. Her opponent in the riding of Vancouver-Centre was then Progressive Conservative Prime Minister Kim Campbell. This riding had a large gay and lesbian population. Hedy promised in her campaign that, if she were elected, she would "fight for a sexual orientation amendment to the human rights legislation."

Hedy defeated Ms. Campbell by four thousand votes. Hedy proved that the human rights issue was more than an election promise when she said, "It is a promise that will be kept."

On December 3, 1993, Dr. Hedy Fry was appointed Parliamentary Secretary to the Minister of Health by Prime Minister Jean Chrétien. On January 25, 1996, Prime Minister Chrétien appointed her Secretary of State for Multiculturalism and the Status of Women.

As a Cabinet Minister, Hedy is a part of the inner circle that brings about change. This appointment was a personal achievement that has brought her satisfaction as a politician. Hedy recalls that she has always been politically-minded. She also remembers campaigning for the first time with her grandmother, in Trinidad.

A reporter asked Hedy what the future held for "the status of women." She responded, "First and foremost we need to be given equal opportunity to play an equal role in society."

Sunera Thobani, former President of the National Action Committee, said about Hedy, "She has been more respectful and available to women's groups than others before her. The first thing she did was to organize a connection with women's groups .... It's absolutely a different experience from before."

Hedy's assessment of her performance in Ottawa has been realistic. She has said, "I strive to be excellent because of my own personal sense of wanting to do my best. I'm outspoken; I've tried to stand up for things I believe in."

### Secretary of State for Multiculturalism and the Status of Women

Hedy has said, "Multiculturalism is the key to Canadian unity. We must understand that people of different races can have a strong sense of belonging to one nation while maintaining their original cultural identities. In this time of globalization, Canada is poised to move to the forefront .... Where I come from (Trinidad), there are many different ethnic people. I am multi-ethnic and multicultural."

Some of the Opposition parties, especially the Reform Party and the Bloc Québécois, say that multiculturalism is divisive and suggest that Hedy's job should be eliminated, for the good of the country. In response to these suggestions, Hedy addressed the Committee on Canadian Heritage. She said that Canada had tried to create a "stir-fry" rather than a "melting pot." Hedy added, "Multiculturalism and respect for our differences are important reasons why this country has been ranked as the best nation in the world by the United Nations." She pointed out that Canada was "the most integrated society in the world."

At a Canada Day celebration in Vancouver (1995). *Courtesy of the office of Hedy Fry, M.D., M.P.*

Hedy concluded, "twenty-five years of multiculturalism has been beneficial to Canada."

In British Columbia, Hedy assured her constituents that the British Columbian caucus was "pushing the envelope" and manoeuvring for change. She said that the six Liberal Members of Parliament from British Columbia worked well together.

Hedy's political colleagues regard her as being politically shrewd, extremely ambitious, and even difficult. However, her constituents say that nobody questions her sincerity.

## THE CABINET

The Prime Minister chooses the Cabinet Ministers that make up the Cabinet. These Ministers are responsible for important areas of government, such as health, law, labour, transportation, and fisheries.

It is customary to have every province and territory represented in the Cabinet. However, if a province does not have an elected Member of Parliament from the governing party, this custom will be broken.

### Privy Councillors

Privy Councillors are appointed by the Governor General on the advice of the Prime Minister. All Cabinet Ministers must become members of the Queen's Privy Council for Canada. Membership is for life, unless the Councillor is dismissed by the Governor General on the advice of the Prime Minister.

### Advice to Young People

Hedy advises young people to participate in building their futures. For example, by joining their school debating teams and / or race relations committees. Involvement in such activities cultivates self-esteem and fosters greater understanding and tolerance of other ethnic groups.

Hedy also suggests that young people should read about local and world events. Get to know the names and beliefs of local and world leaders. When you vote, do so knowing what your Member of Parliament has done and promises to do. Voting is a way of deciding your future.

"Education takes you beyond your limitations," Hedy has said. An important personal goal for young people, she advises, is to complete their high school diplomas. Then they should pursue post-secondary education.

Hedy believes that young people should take social responsibility for the environment and for helping the disadvantaged in society.

### Canada in the Twenty-first Century

Hedy considers Canada to be a world leader for the following reasons:

1. A strong commitment to peace.

2. Respect for all cultures, races, and religions.

3. The solution of conflict through peaceful resolution.

4. A Constitution that promotes the equality of all individuals and groups. This Constitution also balances the rights of individuals with the best interests of the majority.

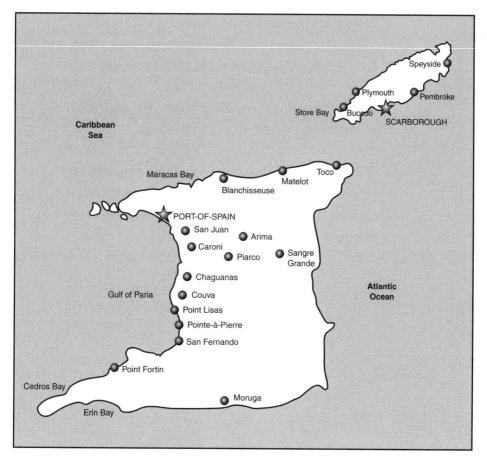

**TRINIDAD AND TOBAGO**

## TRINIDAD AND TOBAGO

It is the last in the chain of islands called the Caribbean. Trinidad and Tobago is situated 10 km (7 mi.) north-east of Venezuela. Trinidad has low mountains. Its area measures 4,828 sq. km (1,864 sq. mi.). It has a population of 1,300,000. Port-of-Spain is its capital. Tobago has a central spine of hills. Its area measures 300 sq. km (116 sq. mi.). It has a population of 50,000. Scarborough is its capital.

*Climate*

The average temperature in Trinidad is 29°C (83°F). Tobago is cooler and less humid. The rainy season is from June to December.

*History and Government*

Trinidad is one of the most cosmopolitan countries in the world. Christopher Columbus claimed Trinidad for Spain in 1498 and the Spaniards settled there in 1592. The British captured Trinidad in 1797 and Tobago in 1814.

After slavery was abolished in 1834, East Indian, and later on Chinese, labourers were brought to the island. Europeans came to Trinidad and Tobago as colonizers; Syrians, as traders. Tobago joined Trinidad as a single unit in 1888. In the 1980s and 1990s, Tobago accepted German and Italian immigrants. Today, these different groups live together peacefully, in the spirit of their nation's motto: Together we aspire; together we achieve.

Trinidad and Tobago became independent from Britain in 1962, and became a republic within the Commonwealth in 1976. The President is the Head of State. The Prime Minister is the head of the government.

*Economy*

Trinidad and Tobago has a strong economy, a well-educated workforce, and a stable democracy. Its diverse range of industries and exports includes oil, natural gas, sugar, cocoa, and coffee.

Because of its leadership role in the Caribbean, Port-of-Spain was chosen in 1995 as the headquarters of the Association of Caribbean States (ACS). The ACS is the twenty-five-nation group that strives to bridge the gap between the English- and Spanish-speaking countries in the Caribbean Sea.

The eighth wonder of the world is in Trinidad. Pitch Lake is an asphalt lake that was discovered by Sir Walter Raleigh in 1595. He used asphalt to cork his leaking ships. The source of this asphalt is embedded under the ocean. When deep cavities are made after drilling for asphalt, the space is gradually replenished within a few days. Asphalt is exported all over the world to cover roads.

*Tourism*

Trinidad and Tobago is the home of the Caribbean Carnival, and is also where calypso and the steel band originated. On Easter Tuesday, the annual Crab and Goat Races take place in Buccoo Village in Tobago. Tourists and villagers come to see the animals and their jockeys reach the finish line.

Tobago is the nature-lover's delight. There are many varieties of plants, birds, and marine life. The beaches are picturesque, with white sand and turquoise waters. The national flower of Trinidad and Tobago is the exotic chaconia. The national birds are Trinidad's elegantly elongated scarlet ibis and Tobago's brown cocrico.

*Education*

The University of the West Indies campus at St. Augustine offers degrees in arts, sciences, and business administration. The faculties of medicine, dentistry, and agriculture are in Trinidad.

# QUOTATIONS

**Dr. Rosemary Brown**

*"The Royal Commission Report on the Status of Women in Canada was tabled in Parliament in 1970. One of the findings was that Canadian women needed to play a much more active role in the political life of the nation. It is not surprising, therefore, that Caribbean women who come out of a tradition of political activism should be motivated by those findings. They choose the political route as their way of building a Canada that is a more equitable and just nation.*

*"This book tells the story of three such women. It demonstrates that it takes the contributions of women of all races, ethnic groups, and cultures, and from every walk of life, to enrich and enhance the quality of life in a country."*

Dr. Rosemary Brown
Lecturer and former New Democratic Party
Member of Parliament for Burnaby-Edmonds
Vancouver, British Columbia

## Tessa Benn-Ireland

*"This biography chronicles the trials and triumphs of three Caribbean Canadian women. Their histories range from colonial days to their present lives as Canadian politicians. Their inspiring stories empower us all to overcome our self-imposed limitations."*

Tessa Benn-Ireland
Author and Librarian
Markham, Ontario

## Dr. Beverley Salmon

*"These women are role models for youth across this country. In spite of their national responsibilities, they have remained loyal to their Caribbean roots. They demonstrate that, through hard work and integrity, they can contribute to Canadian society at the highest levels of government."*

Dr. Beverley Salmon
Former Toronto Councillor
Toronto, Ontario

## Rosemary Sadlier

*"People of African origin have a long history of involvement in Canadian society; from those who first cleared the land and tilled the soil to those who have defended this country. Black women have made strides; from the first woman to found and edit a newspaper in the 1800s, Mary Ann Shadd, to the many Black women, from many backgrounds, who have worked as nurses, teachers, and artists.*

*"Even though these were not the first Black women to have contributed to Canadian society, this book helps to emphasize a crucial concept—that Canadians of African origin have been, are, and will be contributing to Canadian society in a positive way."*

Rosemary Sadlier
Author and President of the
Ontario Black History Society
Toronto, Ontario

# REFERENCES

**Dr. Jean Augustine, M.P.**

The reference to Jean's award is from Cindy
   Reyes's article, "A Most Principled Principal" on
   pages 16, 17, 34, and 35 of the May, 1987 issue of
   *Excellence*.

Jean's quotation regarding her mother and Granny
   is from Cecil Foster's article, "Can Jean Augustine
   Deliver?" on pages 52-56 of the November, 1994
   issue of *Chatelaine*.

Jean's quotation regarding the 1994 South African
   election is from her May 4, 1994 report to the
   House of Commons (Hansard).

Jean's quotations regarding her June 16, 1994
   address to convocation at the University of
   Toronto are from her speaking notes.

Jean's quotations as Chair of an October 4-6, 1994
   OECD high-level conference are from her
   speaking notes.

Jean's quotation regarding Black History Month is
   from her December 14, 1995 motion to the
   House of Commons (Hansard).

**Senator Anne C. Cools**

Rabbi Dr. W. Gunther Plaut's quotation regarding
   Women in Transition, Inc. is from his article,
   "How one woman works to mend lives" in the
   November 3, 1979 edition of the Toronto *Globe
   and Mail*.

Anne's quotation regarding the Speech from the
   Throne is from her January 19, 1994 speech to
   the Senate (Hansard).

The excerpt regarding child battering is from then
   Minister of National Health and Welfare Marc
   Lalonde's 1976 Report, *Child Abuse and Neglect*
   (Hansard).

Anne's quotations regarding violent males are
   from Ron Corbett's article, "Senator finds herself mired in controversy: Radical thought of
   the day" on page 5 of the March 10, 1995
   edition of the Ottawa *Sun*.

The quotation from the editorial on page 24 of the
April 8, 1968 issue of the Manchester *Guardian*
is from Rick Batter and Jean-Guy Carrib's *The
Trudeau Decade*, Doubleday Canada Limited,
Toronto, 1979.

**Hedy Fry, M.D., M.P.**

Hedy's quotations regarding a campaign promise
and women's equality are from a news profile
in the May 13, 1996 edition of the Vancouver
*Sun*.

Sunera Thobani's quotation regarding Hedy is
from a news profile in the May 13, 1996 edition
of the Vancouver *Sun*.

Hedy's quotation regarding her job performance
is from a news profile in the May 13, 1996
edition of the Vancouver *Sun*.

Hedy's quotations regarding multiculturalism are
from Gary Engler's article, "Dr. Fry defends
her job and policies" in the November 19, 1997
edition of the Vancouver *Sun*.

The excerpt from, and copy of, the *Canadian
Charter of Rights and Freedoms* are from pages 14
and 15 of Eugene A. Forsey's *How Canadians
Govern Themselves, 4th Edition*, Canadian
Heritage, Ottawa, 1997.

## Cover Photo Credits

*The three portraits on the front cover are courtesy of the offices of (respectively) Dr. Jean Augustine, M.P., Senator Anne C. Cools, and Hedy Fry, M.D., M.P.*

# INDEX

Peterson, Premier David, 10-11
Pinel, Dr. Philippe, 41
Plaut, Rabbi Dr. W. Gunther, 36, 44
Prayer Book Society of Canada, 49
Prime Minister, 12-14, 21, 24, 36-40, 46, 52, 54-61,
    66-68, 71, 76
Prime Minister of the Century, 58
Princess Stella Sigcan, 19
Privy Council for Canada, The Queen's, 39-40, 71
Privy Councillors, 39-40, 71
Provinces, 14, 45-46, 71

Queen Elizabeth II, 24, 32, 39-40, 45, 51-53, 76

Raleigh, Sir Walter, 76-77
Ryerson Polytechnic Institute.
    *See* Ryerson Polytechnic University
Ryerson Polytechnic University, 35

Sadlier, Rosemary, 22, 81
Salmon, Beverley, xi, 80
Scarlet ibis, 77
Secretary of State, ix-xii, 63, 68-71
Senate of Canada, ix-xii, 27, 35-48
Senator, ix-xii, 27, 35-45, 48-49
Seneca College, 35
Separatism, Quebec, 57
Simon, Olive, 4-5, 15-16
Simon, Ossie, 4